Deviled Eggs

Deviled

Eggs

Debbie Moose

50 Recipes from Simple to Sassy

The Harvard Common Press
Boston, Massachusetts

For Rob,
who knew the job
was dangerous
when he took it

THE HARVARD COMMON PRESS
535 ALBANY STREET
BOSTON, MASSACHUSETTS 02118
www.harvardcommonpress.com

Printed in China

Library of Congress Cataloging-in-Publication Data

Moose, Debbie.
  Deviled eggs : 50 recipes from simple to sassy / Debbie Moose.
    p. cm.
Includes index.
  ISBN 1-55832-272-8 (hc : alk. paper)
  1. Cookery (Eggs) 2. Eggs. I. Title.
  TX745.M66 2004
  641.6'75--dc22

                                        2003022303
ISBN-13: 978-1-55832-272-1

Special bulk-order discounts are available on this and other Harvard
Common Press books. Companies and organizations may purchase books
for premiums or resale, or may arrange a custom edition, by contacting
the Marketing Director at the address above.

10 9

Book design by Deborah Kerner/Dancing Bears Design
Photographs by Duane Winfield
Food styling by Megan Fawn Schlow
Egg timers courtesy of LUX Products Corporation

Contents

acknowledgments

Many dedicated folks offered up their taste buds in support of this book, sampling and critiquing deviled egg recipes that, in some cases, must have made them think I'd lost my mind. If it was a brave man who first ate an oyster, it was a just-as-brave person who first ate a chocolate deviled egg.

Huge thank-yous go to my eaters in Raleigh, North Carolina:

- Anthony Nance, Shelly Kramer, and the other hair stylists (and customers who were unable to flee when I walked in with eggs) at The Elan Group;
- the features department of the *News & Observer* newspaper;
- Martha Waggoner, Sue Wilson, and their compatriots at the Raleigh news bureau of the Associated Press;
- Sheri Green and her fellow staff members at Facility Planning and Construction Management, Wake County Public School System;
- my husband's hungry co-workers at the North Carolina Department of Transportation's Business Systems Improvement Project (yeah, it's a computer geek thing);
- assorted friends and relatives: Lynne Attix, Clara Hager, Becky Westmoreland, Elizabeth Gant, Jo Ann Williford, Karen Megna, Tom Attaway, Neighbor Bill and his buddy Tank, Carol Vatz, Joel Rosch, Jacob Rosch, and Joel Vatz;
- Jan Dorsey at the North Carolina Egg Association, who was a fount of information and assistance.

I'm grateful to those who kindly allowed me to share their recipes in this book: Ana Sortun of Oleana restaurant in Cambridge, Massachusetts; Ben Barker of Magnolia Grill in Durham, North Carolina, and his publisher, the University of North Carolina Press in Chapel Hill, North Carolina; Scott Jones and Todd Erickson of Gourmet a go-go in Dallas, Texas (and their helpful publicist Suzanne Gentry); the American Egg Board; and the California Avocado Commission.

How many ways can I say "thank you"? I have to think of one for my e-mail pal Sharon Christian Aderman in Topeka, Kansas, for her decorating tips. Nancy Olson of Quail Ridge Books in Raleigh (the best bookstore this side of Alpha Centauri) connected me with Sharon and deserves a big load of thanks.

And more thank-yous to:

- editor Pam Hoenig and everyone at The Harvard Common Press;
- Alicia Ross for her advice and support, and for hooking me up with my energetic agent, Carla Glasser of the Betsy Nolan Literary Agency;
- Rose Dosti and Mimi Gormezano for their encouragement.

Finally, I want to thank the Dr. Phil show, the Turner Classic Movies channel, Jimmy Buffett, and the geniuses of Motown for providing entertainment to devil eggs by.

introduction

Deviled eggs are the perfect food. The springy blandness of the whites contrasts perfectly in taste, texture, and color with any filling. There's just enough fat involved to coat the tongue and satisfy the soul. My grandmother created deviled eggs with a filling as silky smooth as whipped cream that had an interesting tart flavor from a combination of vinegar and mustard. For a chunkier bite, add minced items, such as pickles or olives, and less mayo. Go rich by adding blue cheese or caviar, or fire up the afterburners with chiles or hot sauce or both. The range of flavors is practically endless.

On Sunday dinner tables, at family reunions, and at church potlucks, there may be more than one kind of deviled egg being offered up. Hungry folks stake out the plates from those cooks known for the finest deviled eggs, even daring to sneak one or two eggs before grace is said. And a cook is proud (although she has the good manners not to show it) if her plate empties before the competition's.

Deviled eggs have been a favorite take-along dish because most cooks have the necessary ingredients at home. They're simple and quick. Really, if you can boil water, you can have a plate of deviled eggs within half an hour. Their flavor improves with a few hours (or up to a day) in the refrigerator, so you can make them ahead and be ready to go.

When it is possible to find deviled eggs in restaurants, they tend to be categorized as salads or side dishes. But deviled eggs can take on many roles. Add caviar or smoked salmon to the fill-

ing, or pipe it through a cake-decorating tube to give a fancy look, and you have an elegant appetizer. Put them next to a hearty salad or include them as part of a vegetable plate, and they become a filling light brunch. With meat-free stuffings, they're a great option for vegetarian repasts.

Few things on the table are as satisfying as a cool, creamy deviled egg, especially on a summer day as hot as Hades.

The food phrase "to devil" means to add something spicy and/or hot to the dish. So deviled eggs, technically, should have some zip or a little something from Satan's pantry. When using non-spicy ingredients, the results should be called stuffed eggs, if strictly following food lingo. Most people look at the whole flock as deviled eggs, and that's what I'll call them, too. But flame-free doesn't mean boring.

To guide you as you crack the mysteries of the deviled egg, the 50 recipes in this book will cover the devils you know and the devils you don't.

You may ask: Why deviled eggs, and why now? A single bite of these tempting treats will answer the questions. Now grab your pitchforks and prepare for boarding.

The Hard Facts About Hard-Cooked Eggs

First, some proper terminology. In this book, pre-deviled eggs are called "hard cooked," not "hard boiled." Only film noir detectives are hard boiled. You should never actually boil an egg, unless you want rubbery whites and greenish, tough yolks. Why? It's the miracle of chemistry. The longer and more violently you heat the proteins of the egg, the tighter they cling together and the more water they squeeze out. Hence, that bubbling boil yields eggs as dry as toast. Turning up the heat also allows eggs to fall victim to the hideous Green Yolk Phenomenon. You've seen it— that unappealing olive-drab tinge to an otherwise innocent yolk. The color comes from iron in the yolk combining with sulfur in the white to produce iron sulfide. The longer and hotter the egg cooks, the greater the chance for this reaction to occur.

Are you getting the message yet? Be gentle.

Every cook swears by his or her own way of cooking eggs, and if you ask one how he or she came up with that method, the reply will usually be something logical like, "That's how my mama did it." Until I started working on this book, I myself used directions that I just plucked out of a spicy foods cookbook, with the addition of something my mama used to do: shake each egg before putting it in the pan of water in order to center the yolks.

But I'm here to tell you that random selection and old mamas' tales don't make for the best eggs. I switched to the American Egg Board's suggested cooking method and the results have been outstanding, with creamy, easy-to-blend, green-free yolks and tender whites that never have Goodyear stamped on them.

Here it is: Place the eggs in a saucepan large enough to hold them in a single layer. Cover the eggs with cold water, coming about an inch above the eggs. Place the pan on the heat and bring to a boil. Just when the water hits a full boil, completely remove the pan from the heat and slap on the lid. Let the eggs sit, covered, for 15 minutes. Then, drain immediately, cool under running cold water, and get ready to peel.

About that shaking each egg—nobody I checked with had ever heard of doing that to get centered yolks. And, to be honest, it didn't work as often as it did work. Researchers say that the only way to get the most consistently centered yolks is to store the eggs on their sides. Cooking eggs upright in the water—racks are sold for this purpose—also works. But the easiest thing to do if you want perfect bull's-eyes for your devilish fillings is to turn your carton of eggs on its side in the refrigerator the night before you plan to cook them.

You can also buy an electric egg cooker, which hard-cooks seven or eight eggs at a time by steaming them with a small amount of water poured into the base. It's easy—just push a button and come back when the buzzer goes off. If you have space on your kitchen counter for an appliance that cooks only eggs, go for it. I'm not inclined to give up precious space to a single-use appliance, so I'll stick with the stovetop method. These cookers might be useful if you want to get children involved in cooking— they won't have to be near big pots of hot water.

When they're done, cool the eggs immediately under cold running water—5 minutes under the spigot isn't too long—or plunge them into a bowl of ice. The faster you cool the eggs, the less likely you are to face green yolks.

Unpeeled hard-cooked eggs will keep in the refrigerator for

one week. Seal them in a plastic bag to keep them from picking up off flavors or odors (egg shells are porous), and you can devil at a moment's notice.

And a discussion of storage brings us to one of the prime reasons many people try their hands at deviling: to use up their kids' dyed Easter eggs. Food safety experts turn as green as that plastic Easter grass when this subject comes up. Their advice is, in short, forget it. Hard-cooked eggs are safe at room temperature for about two hours. Figure in the time the Easter Bunny needs to hide the eggs in Grandma's sunny, warm yard and how long it takes little Jennifer and Trey to locate them and be photographed holding their cute Easter baskets, and you are way into the danger zone. If the waste appalls you, buy plastic eggs for hiding and save the fresh ones for deviling with special Easter decorating touches, which I'll mention later.

The next preliminary step on the road to hellacious good eating is peeling. As I hit the triple digits on eggs while testing recipes for this book, I thought some enterprising person should devise an egg-peeling machine—for which I would pay any amount. But until science advances, we are left with the manual approach. And there's really no secret to easy peeling. It's a guessing game.

Extremely fresh eggs are the most difficult to peel, and it has to do with egg anatomy. There's an air cell between the shell and the egg in the top of the large ends of eggs. In very fresh eggs, the cell is very small, hence there's little space to get a fingerhold and start peeling smoothly. As the egg ages, the air cell gets bigger. But let things go too long, and you have dried-out eggs. Experts suggest aiming for eggs that are about a week to 10 days old for the combination of good quality and easier peeling.

Crackle the shell all over by rolling it between your hands or gently rolling it against a counter. Don't press too hard, or you'll drive shell into the egg and cut it. Some people put the eggs back in the pot and shake hard, so that the eggs run into each other and the sides of the pot, cracking and loosening the shells. Then, start at the large end, hope for a good-sized air cell, and have patience. Peeling under running water can help wash away bits of shell stuck to the egg.

Most people cut hard-cooked eggs lengthwise—the classic oval sailboat shape—to remove the yolks for deviling. There are those who go against the grain and bisect the eggs through the middle. I try to be tolerant of diverse opinions, but that approach makes no sense to me. To get them to stand up, you have to cut a little slice off the bottom of the white, and that's just another step standing between hungry me and my deviled eggs. Those bisected eggs also don't look attractive at all in my deviled egg plates. But if you swing that way, knock yourself out. They'll still taste good.

dancing with the devils

a s I talked to people and came up with recipes for this book, I found that many folks have definite opinions about their deviled eggs—the texture, the presence (or absence) of chunky things, the type of mayonnaise used. Except in the chunkier recipes, I have aimed for a medium-to-creamy texture. But if you prefer a creamier or drier egg filling, you can play with the amount of mayo or sour cream to get the mouth feel you like. If you add either, you may have to up the spices and flavorings in a particular recipe. Use the recipes as a starting point for your own explorations of the underworld.

I used regular, reduced-fat, and fat-free mayonnaise, plus regular and reduced-fat sour cream, interchangeably with no real differences in the flavors or textures. The lower-fat items do taste and feel different on their own, but when you get other flavorings and spices involved, the differences practically vanish. So it's your call.

However, do not use salad dressing (such as Miracle Whip) in place of mayo—the sweet flavor and thin texture are completely unlike mayo and will not give you the same result. Likewise, using mayo if the recipe asks for salad dressing will give you a different taste and consistency than what was intended.

For The Yolk's on You (page 48), I experimented with substituting drained silken tofu for the egg yolks. Honestly, I am not a tofu fan, but those I know who are thought it was a tasty alternative. If you're more into bean curd than I am, you could experiment with using tofu in other deviled egg recipes.

Any ingredients with liquid—salsa, pickle relish, capers, pickled jalapeños, etc.—should be well drained before you add them so that you don't end up with runny fillings. If you like the flavor of the juice, you can carefully add some back in.

Whatever you put in the fillings, the results often taste better if you allow the deviled eggs time to chill well so that the flavors will blend. If you can't resist temptation, go ahead and enjoy the eggs right away, but try to allow them to chill at least four hours or overnight. All good things are worth waiting for (well, at least that's what Mama said).

there is life beyond paprika

ost folks' efforts to enhance the beauty of deviled eggs extend no further than the jar of paprika on the spice rack. However, the right look can lift a deviled egg from the lowly world of the church picnic into the universe of haute hors d'oeuvres. Just a bit of parsley or a slice of olive will often do to make them jewels for the eyes as well as the appetite. Let the flavor of your filling be a guide to the garnish.

If the filling doesn't contain a lot of large chunky things, you

15

can pipe it into the whites with an elegant swoop. You don't even need special equipment, although if you have star tips and icing bags from a fling with cake decorating, by all means use them. Otherwise, pack the stuffing into a heavy plastic bag and snip off a bit of one corner, then press the filling through the hole into the whites, swirling a bit as you go. To make sure your gems stay picture perfect on their way to the party, transport the stuffing (in the unclipped bag) and whites separately, then snip and fill when ready to serve.

For deviled eggs that look ready to par-tay, give the whites a tie-dyed look. Gently crack or craze the shells of hard-cooked eggs, but don't remove them. Place the eggs in a mixture of vinegar, hot water, and food coloring, as if you were dyeing eggs for Easter. Let them sit for a while so that the color will penetrate the cracks, 30 minutes to an hour. Then, drain on racks or paper towels and peel to reveal the crazy colors.

Like fashions at the Oscars, you can go as far with putting on the devils as you like. Sharon Christian Aderman, a food writer in Topeka, Kansas, and deviled egg fiend, shared with me some of her decorating techniques. For Easter bunnies, she puts the deviled egg halves back together and slices a sliver off the large end so the egg will stand up. She uses pieces of zucchini, pressed into the top of the egg, for ears and slivers of jicama or squash for whiskers, with sunflower seeds, raisins, or whole cloves for eyes. For snowmen, she adorns the joined halves with black olives for hats and pieces of carrot for noses, then sets them on a plate covered with coconut. In summer, she uses the shape of the deviled egg halves to make boats with white paper sails attached to toothpicks.

There was a time when every young woman received a deviled egg plate as a wedding gift. These plates have varying numbers (usually 12) of oval spots into which the halves snuggle perfectly. Plates range from simple glass or crystal to whimsical ceramic. I have one shaped like a chicken. If you fall in love with deviled eggs, I suggest you hie thyself forth to look for a deviled egg plate—they just make the eggs look so pretty. New ones are out there, or try flea markets for vintage ones.

Another kind of plate that works is the olive tray. Long, narrow and shallow, it holds the eggs together attractively without allowing too much movement.

But don't despair if you must use a dinner plate. You just need to make some adjustments. On a naked flat plate, the devils will loll around like lazy manatees, smearing their filling all over each other in a most unattractive manner. Line the plate with something to both hold the eggs steady and make a nice presentation. Try one or a combination of the following: curly lettuce, shredded carrot, shredded red cabbage, watercress, curly parsley, or branches of fresh herbs (oregano, rosemary, mint, lemon balm, basil, or others). Or swipe the plastic grass from the kids' baskets for an Easter display, scattering jellybeans for more color.

deviled eggs for the masses

deviled egg recipes are easily divided or multiplied to feed as few or as many as you like. If you're deviling eggs for dozens rather than for a few close friends, you may want to enlist the help of a power tool. A food processor makes combining large amounts of ingredients fast and easy. If the recipe has chunky ingredients that are important for the filling's texture, be sure to stir them in at the end by hand.

Deviled eggs, if properly refrigerated, will be safe to eat for as long as other leftovers—three or four days. However, the quality may suffer, because the filling can dry out in the refrigerator. To ensure the best flavor, it's probably best not to prepare deviled eggs for parties more than two days ahead, and wrap them up securely in plastic wrap.

Now get cracking on a whole new world of deviled eggs!

good old eggs

Take a trip down memory lane with the traditional deviled eggs of the past. Here are eggs like the ones your grandmother made for Sunday dinner, along with some interesting variations. Need to scare up a last-minute dish for an office party? Look here for quick recipes, using ingredients that you can always keep on hand, that will make it look like you worked all day.

ma-ma's deviled eggs

My grandmother Ruth Link Shaw of Statesville, North Carolina, kept a perfect house and made perfect food while wearing aprons that covered her whole body like welder's garb—not that she ever got a spot on one of them. And she never wanted anyone to know exactly how she produced those divine pound cakes and crispy fried chicken, so she never wrote down a recipe. But you can't keep a good deviled egg secret, so I re-created her tart, creamy treats from my memory and from talking with other members of my family. You should make these very smooth, just like my Ma-Ma did.

6 hard-cooked eggs, peeled, cut in half, and yolks
  mashed in a bowl
2 tablespoons plus 2 teaspoons mayonnaise
1 tablespoon prepared yellow mustard
2 teaspoons distilled white vinegar
$1/4$ teaspoon salt, or to taste
$1/4$ teaspoon black pepper, or to taste
Paprika for garnish

1. Combine the thoroughly mashed yolks and mayonnaise, then stir in the mustard and vinegar. Stir in the salt and pepper, then taste and adjust if necessary. Stir well with a spoon to achieve a creamy texture.

2. Fill the whites evenly with the mixture and garnish each egg half with paprika.

Makes 12

cousin judy's deviled eggs

My cousin Judy Ross in Asheville, North Carolina, likes her deviled eggs tart and smooth. And, above all, she says, "No pickle relish. Yuk." These are good eating while Judy and her husband are watching a NASCAR race.

6 hard-cooked eggs, peeled, cut in half, and yolks
   mashed in a bowl

2 tablespoons mayonnaise

2 teaspoons prepared yellow mustard

2 teaspoons Worcestershire sauce

$3/4$ teaspoon Old Bay seasoning

1 teaspoon distilled white or cider vinegar

$1/4$ teaspoon black pepper

Salt to taste

Paprika for garnish

1. Combine the thoroughly mashed yolks with the mayonnaise and mustard. Stir in the Worcestershire, Old Bay, vinegar, and pepper. With the Worcestershire and Old Bay, the filling is pretty salty already, but taste and add more salt if you need it.

2. Fill the whites evenly with the mixture and garnish each egg half with a sprinkle of paprika.

Makes 12

eggstraordinary!

Heard of egg candling? Long ago, an actual candle was used to see inside the egg so that it could be graded for quality. Today, eggs pass on rollers over high-intensity electric lights, which allow workers (still called candlers) to check for imperfections.

pimento cheese
deviled eggs

G rowing up as a Southerner, pimento cheese was my peanut butter—the satisfying food that we always had in the house for when the hungries struck. This may be my ultimate comfort food deviled egg, combining two of my favorite goodies in one.

6 hard-cooked eggs, peeled, cut in half, and yolks
   mashed in a bowl
1/4 cup finely shredded sharp cheddar cheese
1 tablespoon plus 1 teaspoon drained and
   chopped pimentos
2 tablespoons mayonnaise
2 teaspoons Dijon mustard
2 teaspoons chopped Vidalia or other sweet onion
1/2 teaspoon grated garlic
Salt and black pepper to taste
Chopped pimentos for garnish

1. Combine the thoroughly mashed yolks with the cheddar, pimentos, mayonnaise, mustard, onion, and garlic. Taste, then season with salt and pepper.

2. Fill the whites evenly with the mixture and garnish each egg half with chopped pimentos.

Makes 12

eggstraordinary!

Eggshells are so porous that they will allow the egg to absorb flavors from nearby items. Placing a truffle or, less pleasantly, an onion, in or near the carton will infuse the eggs with that flavor.

ann's midwestern-style deviled eggs

I got this recipe from my friend Ann Berry, one of a group of women that I regularly have lunch with. These wise women have purses older than I am and make retirement look like a blast (although many of my office-bound friends consider hanging around the house deviling eggs the same as retirement). Ann's mother-in-law—like Ann, a native Kansan—came up with the original recipe. This one includes Ann's embellishments, plus her insistence on using salad dressing instead of mayo.

6 hard-cooked eggs, peeled, cut in half, and yolks
   mashed in a bowl
2 tablespoons salad dressing, such as Miracle Whip
1 1/2 teaspoons prepared yellow mustard
2 teaspoons cider vinegar
1 1/2 teaspoons light brown sugar
1/2 teaspoon garlic powder
2 teaspoons chopped green onion (white and green parts)
   or fresh chives, plus more for garnish
Salt and black pepper to taste

1. Combine the thoroughly mashed yolks with the salad dressing and mustard. Stir in the vinegar, brown sugar, garlic powder, and green onion. Taste, then season with salt and pepper.

2. Fill the whites evenly with the mixture and garnish each egg half with a sprinkle of chopped green onion.

Makes 12

hollyann's stop-the-music deviled eggs

T he bluegrass pickers gathered for their weekly old-time music session at May's Store in Christian Light, North Carolina, drop their banjos when HollyAnn Rogers arrives with these goodies. HollyAnn says the secret is using chow-chow instead of the same old pickle relish. Chow-chow is spicy and mustardy and contains a variety of finely chopped vegetables instead of the standard cucumbers. "I use the chow-chow my mama puts up, but you can find it in country stores, too," HollyAnn says. "I never have any leftovers!"

6 hard-cooked eggs, peeled, cut in half, and yolks
   mashed in a bowl
$^1/_4$ cup mayonnaise
2 tablespoons chow-chow
2 teaspoons prepared yellow mustard
$^1/_4$ teaspoon salt
$^1/_8$ to $^1/_4$ teaspoon black pepper, to your taste
Paprika for garnish

1. Combine the thoroughly mashed yolks and mayonnaise until fairly smooth. Mix in the chow-chow, mustard, salt, and pepper.

2. Fill the whites evenly with the mixture and sprinkle each egg half generously with paprika.

Makes 12

eggstraordinary!

Greek mythology says that Castor and Pollux, the twins of the astrological sign Gemini, came from an egg rather than being born.

dippy eggs

My Aunt Pauline Ross used to make a dip that was beloved in her family, even if it was a bit aromatic. It's the inspiration for these eggs. Use a microplane grater, if you have one. Serve with Tic Tacs on the side.

6 hard-cooked eggs, peeled, cut in half, and yolks
   mashed in a bowl
5 tablespoons plus 1 teaspoon whipped cream cheese
2 teaspoons mayonnaise
1 tablespoon grated onion with juice
$1/2$ teaspoon grated garlic with juice
$1/2$ teaspoon black pepper, plus more for garnish
Salt to taste

1. Combine the thoroughly mashed yolks with the cream cheese and mayonnaise. Add the grated onion and garlic and their juices to the mixture and blend in the pepper. Taste, then season with salt.

2. Fill the whites evenly with the mixture and garnish each egg half with pepper.

Makes 12

eggstraordinary!

The 215 milligrams of cholesterol each egg contains put it on the bad-food list until further research showed that the culprit in any diet is the amount of saturated fat consumed, not the cholesterol. Since there are only 1.5 grams of saturated fat in one egg, enjoy.

yo' mama's deviled eggs

Who makes the best deviled eggs? Why, yo' mama, of course. Here, I re-create the basic mayonnaise-y, paprika-y flavors everyone thinks of in deviled eggs. Since my own mother was allergic to eggs, I grew up virtually devil-less. Could that be why I have spent my life in pursuit of the perfect deviled egg? And if these aren't just like yo' mama's, well, go get that recipe from her yourself.

6 hard-cooked eggs, peeled, cut in half, and yolks
    mashed in a bowl
$1/4$ cup plus 1 teaspoon mayonnaise
$2 1/2$ teaspoons Dijon mustard (use yellow mustard
    if you prefer a milder flavor)
$1/4$ teaspoon garlic powder
1 tablespoon sweet pickle relish, drained
Salt and black pepper to taste
Paprika for garnish

1. Combine the thoroughly mashed yolks with the mayonnaise. Blend in the mustard, garlic powder, and relish. Taste, then season with salt and pepper.

2. Fill the whites evenly with the mixture and garnish each egg half with paprika.

Makes 12

eggstraordinary!

Central Europeans have a long tradition of elaborately decorated Easter eggs. The Poles and Ukrainians even today draw intricate designs on the shells with a wax pencil and dip the eggs in multiple colors to create true works of art.

six dashing devils

You just never know when you're going to want to devil eggs. While I, of course, am prepared at all times for such deviled egg emergencies as, say, an impromptu margarita party at the pool, I am aware that others may need a jump start. Here are six quick ways to amaze your friends using stuff you can keep in the pantry and fridge all the time.

6 hard-cooked eggs, peeled, cut in half, and yolks
 mashed in a bowl
2 tablespoons plus 2 teaspoons sour cream
2 tablespoons plus 2 teaspoons mayonnaise

Combine the thoroughly mashed yolks with the sour cream and mayonnaise. Then blend in one of the following seasonings:

- *1 tablespoon salt-free garlic and herb seasoning*
- *1 tablespoon plus 1 ½ teaspoons dry cream of spinach soup and dip mix*
- *1 tablespoon plus 1 ½ teaspoons Mrs. Dash Extra Spicy Seasoning*
- *1 tablespoon plus 1 teaspoon dry ranch dressing mix*
- *1 tablespoon plus 1 teaspoon dry dill dip mix*
- *1 tablespoon plus 1 ½ teaspoons taco seasoning*

Taste the mixture, then season with salt and pepper, if needed — most dip mixes are salty enough. Fill the whites evenly with the mixture. Garnish the halves, if you want to fuss, with a little chopped fresh Italian parsley or chives, or a sprinkle of paprika. Try a little nutmeg on the spinach soup mix eggs.

Makes 12

springtime herb delights

These fresh little devils come out looking as pretty as the first azaleas of spring. Don't let any stems slip in while you're chopping the herbs very finely—you don't want to chomp down on a big woody thing.

6 hard-cooked eggs, peeled, cut in half, and yolks
   mashed in a bowl
$1/4$ cup mayonnaise
$1 1/2$ teaspoons fresh lemon juice
1 tablespoon finely chopped fresh Italian parsley
$1/2$ teaspoon finely chopped fresh dill
2 teaspoons finely chopped fresh chives
Salt and black pepper to taste
Fresh Italian parsley leaves for garnish

1. Combine the thoroughly mashed yolks with the mayonnaise and lemon juice. Stir in the finely chopped herbs. Taste, then season with salt and pepper.

2. Fill the whites evenly with the mixture and garnish each egg half with a whole parsley leaf.

Makes 12

eggstraordinary!

From the earliest civilizations, eggs were seen as symbols of the renewal of life. Early Christians adopted the egg as a symbol of Christ's resurrection.

eggstraordinary!

Eggs contain very high-quality protein, which is why they're classified with meat in food pyramids. Protein-wise, one egg is equal to one ounce of lean meat, fish, or poultry.

eggstraordinary!

A roasted egg is part of the Passover Seder plate, symbolizing for Jews the ancient sacrificial offering of a roasted animal to God on holidays.

saucy salad eggs

The TV commercials tell us to drink our veggies, but I'd rather eat them in a deviled egg. And it allows you to feel so virtuously healthy. A spring brunch would be a perfect setting for these little jewels. Change the flavor by substituting an herb-flavored vinegar.

1 tablespoon plus 2 teaspoons grated carrot
6 hard-cooked eggs, peeled, cut in half, and yolks
    mashed in a bowl
$1/4$ cup mayonnaise
1 tablespoon Dijon mustard
1 teaspoon white wine vinegar
$1/2$ teaspoon garlic powder
1 tablespoon plus 2 teaspoons chopped green bell pepper
2 tablespoons plus 1 teaspoon chopped onion
1 teaspoon chopped fresh Italian parsley
Salt and black pepper to taste
Fresh Italian parsley leaves for garnish

1. Let the grated carrot drain on several layers of paper towels for a few minutes, pressing lightly, to remove excess moisture.

2. Combine the thoroughly mashed yolks with the mayonnaise and mustard. Stir in the vinegar, garlic powder, green pepper, onion, parsley, and drained carrot. Taste, then season with salt and pepper.

3. Fill the whites evenly with the mixture and garnish each egg half with a parsley leaf.

Makes 12

slightly cracked

F ar out, silky smooth, or just plain different, it's all here. Don't get the yolk? Then it can disappear with tofu in its place. And drop your pickle relish fantasies to enjoy dessert eggs and warm appetizer-style recipes.

Double Devils

Green Eggs and Ham

Blue Devils

Egg's Got a Secret

It's Not Delivered, It's de Devils

Avocado Angel Eggs

Gourmet a go-go's Conversation
     Pit Barbecue Deviled Eggs

Saturday Night Eggs

Spinach-Bacon Deviled Eggs

The Yolk's on You

Chick in a Blanket

Satan's Skins

Devil's Food Eggs

Ambrosias

Strawberry Cheesecakes
     on the Half Shell

double devils

I f one little devil is good, two are twice as nice for this treat using canned deviled ham.

6 hard-cooked eggs, peeled, cut in half, and yolks
    mashed in a bowl
2 tablespoons plus 2 teaspoons mayonnaise
1 teaspoon prepared yellow mustard
1 tablespoon plus 2 teaspoons deviled ham
2 teaspoons chopped black olives
1 1/4 teaspoons capers, drained
Salt and black pepper to taste
Black olive slices for garnish

1. Combine the thoroughly mashed yolks with the mayonnaise and mustard. Stir in the deviled ham, olives, and capers. Taste, then season with salt and pepper.

2. Fill the whites evenly with the mixture and garnish each egg half with an olive slice.

Makes 12

eggstraordinary!

Some say an egg will stand on its small end on the vernal equinox.

green eggs and ham

You could eat them in a house, or you could eat them with a mouse. But you will like these green eggs and ham, Sam I am . . . sure. Perfect for St. Patrick's Day or Easter.

About 2 teaspoons green food coloring, or enough
   to color the whites
6 hard-cooked eggs, peeled, cut in half, and yolks
   mashed in a bowl
$^1/_4$ cup plus 2 teaspoons mayonnaise
1 tablespoon plus 1 teaspoon prepared yellow mustard
$^1/_4$ cup finely chopped cooked country ham
Salt and black pepper to taste

1. Pour the green food coloring on a plate and gently roll the egg white halves in it. (Your fingers will turn very green, but this is the best way to get a vivid color.) Place the whites, hollow side down, on a cake rack over a plate or tray to let drip-dry.

2. While the whites dry, mix the thoroughly mashed yolks with the mayonnaise, mustard, and ham until well combined. Taste, then season with salt and pepper.

3. Before filling them with the mixture, gently dab the whites with paper towels to remove excess coloring, if necessary.

Makes 12

blue devils

The Duke University Blue Devils are my alma mater's arch rival in basketball, but sometimes you have to give the devils their due. The unusual flavor makes this a good appetizer or cocktail hour munchie. Fry up some bacon for the topping or use the real bacon bits available in a jar—avoid the fakin' bacon.

6 hard-cooked eggs, peeled, cut in half, and yolks
  mashed in a bowl
2 tablespoons plus 2 teaspoons mayonnaise
1 teaspoon Dijon mustard
2 tablespoons crumbled blue cheese
Salt and black pepper to taste
About 3 tablespoons real bacon bits

1. Combine the thoroughly mashed yolks with the mayonnaise and mustard. Add the blue cheese and mash well into the mixture with a spoon. Taste, then season with salt and pepper.

2. Fill the whites evenly with the mixture and garnish each egg half with the bacon bits.

Makes 12

eggstraordinary!

In Austria, some still follow the practice of throwing a blessed egg off the roof of a house and burying it where it strikes the ground in order to protect the house from lightning.

eggs' got a secret

Who doesn't like a little surprise? Pump up the chili powder if you want more spice in these mysterious salty-sweet devils.

6 hard-cooked eggs, peeled, cut in half, and yolks
    mashed in a bowl
1 tablespoon plus 2 teaspoons salad dressing, such as
    Miracle Whip
2 tablespoons plus 2 teaspoons mayonnaise
2 teaspoons prepared yellow mustard
1/2 teaspoon hot chili powder
Salt and black pepper to taste
12 pimento-stuffed green olives, drained well

1. Combine the thoroughly mashed yolks with the salad dressing, mayonnaise, mustard, and chili powder. Taste, then season with salt and pepper. (Go light on the salt, since the olives are salty.)

2. Dab the olives with paper towel to remove excess juice. Place one whole olive in each egg white half, then cover with the filling mixture, gently pressing it in and mounding it up to hide the olive.

Makes 12

eggstraordinary!

It was customary for peasants in central Europe to rub eggs on their plows as a fertility ritual to improve their spring crops.

it's not delivered,
it's de devils

Pizza with everything (except those nasty anchovies) in an egg. You can throw these babies together faster than you can sing "O Sole Mio." Get the best kind of Italian herb blend you can find, with no salt.

6 hard-cooked eggs, peeled, cut in half, and yolks
   mashed in a bowl
$1/4$ cup plus 2 teaspoons mayonnaise
1 teaspoon prepared yellow mustard
2 tablespoons plus 2 teaspoons chopped pepperoni
$1/2$ teaspoon Italian herb blend seasoning
1 teaspoon chopped onion
$1/2$ teaspoon freshly grated Parmesan cheese,
   plus more for garnish
Salt and black pepper to taste

1. Combine the thoroughly mashed yolks with the mayonnaise and mustard. Stir in the pepperoni, Italian seasoning, onion, and Parmesan. Taste, then season with salt and pepper.

2. Fill the whites evenly with the mixture and garnish each egg half with a light sprinkling of Parmesan.

Makes 12

avocado angel eggs

T hese devils go green when creamy avocado takes the place of the yolks in this recipe from the California Avocado Commission. With that smooth, filling flavor of the avocado, you won't miss the yolks, or the mayo.

2 ripe California avocados
1 tablespoon fresh lemon juice
1/4 teaspoon garlic powder
2 tablespoons finely chopped shallots or green onions
2 teaspoons capers (optional), drained and mashed
12 hard-cooked eggs, peeled, cut in half, and yolks discarded or set aside for another use
Slivers of red, yellow, or green bell pepper for garnish

1. Cut the avocados in half, remove the pits, peel, and cut into cubes. Place in a medium-size bowl, add the lemon juice and garlic powder, and mash to blend. Stir in the shallots and capers, if using.

2. Fill the whites evenly with the avocado mixture and garnish each egg half with bell pepper slivers.

Makes 24

eggstraordinary!

Hens fed on alfalfa, grass, and yellow corn produce eggs with lighter-colored yolks than do wheat-fed hens.

gourmet a go-go's conversation pit barbecue deviled eggs

They say everything's bigger in Texas, and that's true with the flavors of this recipe from Gourmet a go-go in Dallas. Proprietor Scott Jones offers gourmet takeout and catering of dishes that have their roots in good old American comfort food but branch out into new flavors. And he's a big fan of deviled eggs—the menu offers 10 different kinds. Visit Gourmet a go-go at 5219 West Lover's Lane, Dallas, Texas.

12 hard-cooked eggs, peeled, cut in half, and yolks removed
4 ounces (half an 8-ounce package) cream cheese
$1/2$ cup mayonnaise
2 tablespoons prepared yellow mustard
$1/4$ cup of your favorite barbecue sauce
1 teaspoon minced garlic
$1 1/2$ cups chopped cooked smoked beef brisket (see Note)
$1/3$ cup minced Texas 1015 or other sweet onion
$1/3$ cup minced dill pickles
Salt and black pepper to taste
Barbecue sauce in a squeeze bottle and finely
    chopped fresh Italian parsley for garnish

1. In a food processor, process the yolks, cream cheese, mayonnaise, mustard, barbecue sauce, and garlic together until smooth. Transfer to a medium-size bowl and fold in the brisket, onion, and pickles. Taste, then season with salt and pepper.

2. Fill the whites generously with the mixture. Drizzle each egg half with barbecue sauce and sprinkle with parsley.

Makes 24

note: *You can find cooked smoked beef brisket at the deli counters of large supermarkets or at delicatessens. Cooked beef barbecue in sauce is available at some supermarket prepared food areas; if you use it, omit the barbecue sauce in the recipe. You can also use leftover grilled flank steak, but the flavor and texture will be different; add about 1 teaspoon Liquid Smoke to the recipe to adjust the flavor.*

saturday night eggs

Creole mustard is tart and has an interesting texture from whole mustard seeds. Use any kind of bumpy mustard if you can't find Creole. Then just rock and roll on your own Saturday night.

6 hard-cooked eggs, peeled, cut in half, and yolks
    mashed in a bowl
2 tablespoons mayonnaise
2 teaspoons Heinz 57 steak sauce
1 1/2 teaspoons Creole mustard
1 tablespoon plus 1 teaspoon chopped red onion
2 teaspoons chopped pickled jalapeños
Pinch of sugar
Salt and black pepper to taste
Chopped red onion or pickled jalapeños, drained, for garnish

1. Combine the thoroughly mashed yolks with the mayonnaise, steak sauce, mustard, onion, jalapeños, and sugar. Taste, then season with salt and pepper.

2. Fill the whites evenly with the mixture and garnish each egg half with chopped red onion or jalapeños.

MAKES 12

spinach-bacon deviled eggs

Jan Dorsey of the North Carolina Egg Association says that these eggs are particularly tasty. The recipe comes from an association pamphlet.

12 hard-cooked eggs, peeled, cut in half, and yolks
    mashed in a bowl
$^1/_2$ cup frozen chopped spinach, thawed, drained,
    and squeezed dry
$^1/_4$ cup mayonnaise
$^1/_4$ cup real bacon bits
2 $^1/_2$ tablespoons cider vinegar
2 tablespoons butter, softened
1 tablespoon sugar
2 teaspoons black pepper
$^1/_4$ teaspoon salt

1. Combine the thoroughly mashed yolks with the remaining ingredients and mix well.

2. Fill the whites evenly with the mixture.

Makes 24

eggstraordinary!

Besides white, eggshells can be brown or even blue,
depending on the breed of the hen. No matter the color
of the shell, eggs are all the same nutritionally.

the yolk's on you

Now, generally I feel about tofu the same way I feel about rice cakes—I might as well just eat air. But these nontraditional devils, spiced up with plenty of flavorings, are a good way to go if you insist on doing something healthy, like get more soy into your diet. My vegetarian friend Lynne loved them, and she should know from tofu! Be sure to get the silken kind of tofu, which blends smoothly with the other ingredients.

²/₃ cup drained and mashed (see Note) silken tofu
2 tablespoons mayonnaise
1 tablespoon Dijon mustard
1 ¹/₂ teaspoons curry powder
¹/₂ teaspoon garlic powder
2 teaspoons chopped fresh Italian parsley
2 teaspoons chopped onion
Salt and black pepper to taste
6 hard-cooked eggs, peeled, cut in half, and yolks discarded
    or set aside for another use
Fresh Italian parsley leaves for garnish

1. Combine the tofu, mayonnaise, and mustard in a medium-size bowl. Stir in the curry, garlic powder, parsley, and onion. Taste, then season with salt and pepper.

2. Fill the whites evenly with the mixture and garnish each egg half with a parsley leaf.

Makes 12

note: *Place the tofu in a fine-mesh strainer or a colander lined with cheesecloth over a bowl and add a weight to press the liquid from it. (Try putting a layer of plastic wrap over the tofu, then placing another bowl on top containing a can as a weight.) Let drain about 10 minutes, until the tofu is dry. Mash the drained tofu in another bowl.*

chick in a blanket

You remember those little sausages wrapped in dough that we're supposed to be too sophisticated to like anymore? Well, you've noticed which munchie, after the deviled eggs, goes fastest at parties, haven't you? This recipe combines both flavors in one, and most of the work can be done in advance. These appetizer-style deviled eggs should be served warm.

6 hard-cooked eggs, peeled, cut in half, and yolks
   mashed in a bowl

²/₃ cup crumbled cooked hot or mild sausage, drained
   well and cooled to room temperature

2 tablespoons sour cream

2 tablespoons prepared yellow mustard

2 tablespoons chopped onion

¹/₄ teaspoon garlic powder

2 tablespoons plus 2 teaspoons shredded cheddar cheese

6 or 7 drops Tabasco sauce, to your taste

Salt and black pepper to taste

12 triangles refrigerated crescent roll dough (12 rolls worth)

1 egg, lightly beaten

1. Prepare the deviled eggs 4 hours before serving or up to overnight. Combine the thoroughly mashed yolks with the sausage, sour cream, mustard, onion, garlic powder, cheddar, and Tabasco. Taste, then season with salt and pepper.

2. Fill the whites evenly with the mixture, pressing it in firmly. Cover tightly with plastic wrap and refrigerate until ready to use.

3. When ready to serve, remove the deviled eggs from the refrigerator and let sit 10 to 15 minutes to come to room temperature. Preheat the oven according to the crescent roll dough package instructions. Get a nonstick rimmed baking sheet or coat a baking sheet with nonstick cooking spray; set aside. Lay out one triangle of dough with the short side closest to you and the point farthest away. Place a filled egg half lengthwise, filling side up, near the

point and gently pull the point over the top of the egg. Roll the egg in the dough toward you, gently stretching the dough, if necessary, to completely cover the egg. The egg should be completely covered by dough and be filling side up when you're done. Pinch the seam and twist the ends of dough on either side of the egg to seal. Brush lightly with the beaten egg and place on the prepared baking sheet. Repeat with the remaining egg halves and dough triangles. Bake until brown, about 12 minutes. Serve warm.

M a k e s 1 2

satan's skins

This warm appetizer echoes the flavors of that classic munchie, potato skins. Make the eggs ahead of time and cook 'em as you need 'em to keep the party going. Be sure to insulate the filling from the heat by completely covering the tops of the eggs with cheese, and don't let the cheese brown, but just let it get good and gooey. Real bacon bits are available in jars at the supermarket. If you cook your own bacon, be sure to drain it well and let it cool to room temperature before adding to the mixture.

6 hard-cooked eggs, peeled, cut in half, and yolks mashed in a bowl

$^1/_3$ cup real bacon bits

2 tablespoons plus 1 teaspoon sour cream

$^1/_2$ teaspoon Dijon mustard

2 $^1/_2$ teaspoons chopped pickled jalapeños, drained

3 teaspoons chopped fresh chives

1 tablespoon plus 1 teaspoon chopped onion

Salt and black pepper to taste

About $^1/_2$ cup finely shredded cheddar cheese

1. Prepare the deviled eggs 4 hours before serving or up to overnight. Combine the thoroughly mashed yolks with the bacon, sour cream, mustard, jalapeños, chives, and onion. Taste, then season with salt and pepper.

2. Fill the whites evenly with the mixture, pressing it in firmly. Cover tightly with plastic wrap and refrigerate until ready to use.

3. When ready to serve, preheat the oven to 350°F. Get a rimmed nonstick baking sheet or coat a baking sheet with nonstick cooking spray. (The rim is important so the eggs don't roll off.) Place the eggs on the prepared sheet and sprinkle with the cheddar, making sure to cover the tops of the eggs entirely. Bake until the cheese is melted but not brown, 5 to 7 minutes, checking several times. Serve warm.

Makes 12

note: *You can put the eggs under the broiler, but watch very carefully to prevent burning. The cheese will melt in 2 minutes or less, depending on your broiler.*

eggstraordinary!

In ancient cultures, eggs were often buried with the dead to provide nourishment for the journey into the afterlife.

devil's food eggs

I believe chocolate is a basic building block of life, and I'm not about to write a cookbook without including something with chocolate in it. These work, I swear. Try 'em. Adding a drop or two of raspberry liqueur to the filling would just make these eggs something to sell your soul for. It is vitally important to let these come to room temperature before eating them or the filling will be like a rock, so learn some self-restraint.

6 hard-cooked eggs, peeled, cut in half, and yolks
    mashed in a bowl
6 tablespoons (³/₄ stick) unsalted butter, softened
1 tablespoon plus 1 teaspoon crème fraîche
2 teaspoons unsweetened cocoa powder
1 tablespoon firmly packed light brown sugar
Pinch of salt
Grated milk chocolate candy bar for garnish

1. Combine the thoroughly mashed yolks with the butter and crème fraîche—get the mixture as smooth as possible. Add the cocoa, brown sugar, and salt, stirring until well combined.

2. Fill the whites evenly with the mixture and garnish each egg half with grated chocolate.

Makes 12

eggstraordinary!

The Chinese used to try to preserve fresh eggs by immersing them in such things as salt and wet clay, cooked rice, or salt and wood ash mixed with tea.

ambrosias

Oh, get over your pickle relish fixation. Why not dessert deviled eggs? These taste like that lovely cheese ball that everyone can't get to fast enough when it appears on the holiday goodie table.

6 hard-cooked eggs, peeled, cut in half, and yolks
  mashed in a bowl

3 tablespoons whipped cream cheese

2 tablespoons sour cream

2 tablespoons plus 2 teaspoons crushed pineapple,
  drained well

2 teaspoons firmly packed light brown sugar

2 teaspoons chopped pecans

Pinch of salt

Ground nutmeg for garnish

1. Combine the thoroughly mashed yolks with the cream cheese and sour cream. Stir in the pineapple, brown sugar, pecans, and salt.

2. Fill the whites evenly with the mixture and garnish each egg half with a light sprinkle of nutmeg.

Makes 12

eggstraordinary!

The New York soda fountain favorite egg cream contains no eggs at all.

strawberry cheesecakes
on the half shell

L ittle baby cheesecakes and deviled eggs, too. It must be heaven. Take my advice and do not omit the food coloring, or you'll have gray eggs the next day.

6 hard-cooked eggs, peeled, cut in half, and yolks
    mashed in a bowl
3 tablespoons plus 1 teaspoon whipped cream cheese
2 tablespoons sour cream
1 tablespoon strawberry jam
Pinch of salt
Dash of ground nutmeg
About 4 drops of red food coloring
Graham cracker crumbs for garnish

1. Combine the thoroughly mashed yolks with the cream cheese, sour cream, and jam. Stir in the salt and nutmeg, then mix in the red food coloring.

2. Fill the whites evenly with the mixture and garnish each egg half with a sprinkling of graham cracker crumbs.

Makes 12

lucifer goes uptown

These little devils go gourmet with caviar, prosciutto, or smoked salmon. Travel the globe with flavors from India to Italy. No reservations required.

Crabby Eggs

Lox and Eggs

Oleana's Deviled Eggs with Tuna,
    Black Olives, and Tomato

Gourmet a go-go's Betcha
    By Golly Wow Eggs

Pesty Devils

Greek Eggs

Maharajahs

Bella Tuscany

Dirty Martinis

Beelzebub's Bloody Marys

Magnolia Grill's Deviled Eggs
    with Caviar

Sharon's Hot Deviled Eggs

Deviled Eggs Benedict with
    Sheri's 1-2-3 Hollandaise

crabby eggs

J ust like a summer day at the beach, with all that lovely fresh seafood. If you have cooked fresh crab, by all means use it in these cool, mild eggs — in fact, add more!

6 hard-cooked eggs, peeled, cut in half, and yolks
  mashed in a bowl
2 tablespoons mayonnaise
2 tablespoons sour cream
$1/3$ cup chopped cooked crabmeat, picked over
  for shells and cartilage
3 tablespoons plus 1 teaspoon diced avocado
2 teaspoons chopped onion
2 teaspoons capers, drained well
1 teaspoon chopped garlic
1 teaspoon fresh lemon juice
$1/2$ teaspoon celery seeds
Salt and black pepper to taste
Paprika for garnish

1. Combine the thoroughly mashed yolks with the mayonnaise and sour cream. Stir in the crabmeat, avocado, onion, capers, garlic, lemon juice, and celery seeds. Taste, then season with salt and pepper.

2. Fill the whites evenly with the mixture and garnish each egg half with a sprinkling of paprika.

Makes 12

eggstraordinary!

The term "to egg on" came not from the word "egg" but from an Old English word that meant to goad or incite.

lox and eggs

This recipe is inspired by a breakfast dish that my husband loved as a child. When we got married, I was Southern sausage and bacon, he was Jewish lox and bagels. Well, I've finally gotten used to the smoked fish, as long as there aren't any beady-eyed fish heads staring at me over my morning coffee. And here's a tip: With the pink color of the filling and the caper garnish, these devils look gorgeous even if you put them together in your sleep.

> 6 hard-cooked eggs, peeled, cut in half, and yolks
>   mashed in a bowl
> 2 tablespoons sour cream
> 2 teaspoons whipped cream cheese
> 1 1/2 teaspoons Dijon mustard
> 2 tablespoons chopped smoked salmon
> 1 1/2 teaspoons grated onion
> Salt and black pepper to taste
> Drained capers for garnish

1. Combine the thoroughly mashed yolks with the sour cream, cream cheese, and mustard. Stir in the smoked salmon and onion. Taste, then season with salt and pepper.

2. Fill the whites evenly with the mixture and garnish each egg half with 3 or 4 capers.

Makes 12

eggstraordinary!

Native Americans believed that the Great Spirit emerged from a golden egg to create the world.

oleana's deviled eggs with tuna, black olives, and tomato

My publisher said I just had to get this recipe from Oleana restaurant, because the eggs are a staff favorite. How could I refuse—especially when it meant talking to the delightful chef, Ana Sortun? Ana said that Oleana's menu explores Arabic-Mediterranean flavors, especially those of Turkey, although this recipe isn't Turkish. Ana serves these little eggs, a twist on the traditional Spanish tapa, as a bread condiment. Visit Oleana at 134 Hampshire Street, Cambridge, Massachusetts.

1 tablespoon extra-virgin olive oil, plus more for garnish
1 cup minced fresh tuna
1 cup minced celery
1 scallion, minced
Tiny pinch of curry powder
Salt and black pepper to taste
8 hard-cooked eggs, peeled, cut in half, and yolks
    mashed in a bowl
1 cup thick mayonnaise, preferably homemade
1 tablespoon chopped fresh Italian parsley
8 black olives, pitted
1 plum tomato, seeded, finely chopped, and drained

1. In a medium-size saucepan, heat the olive oil over medium heat, then add the tuna, celery, scallion, and curry, season with salt and pepper, and cook, stirring, until just cooked through. Let cool, drain well, and chop again by hand.

2. Combine the thoroughly mashed yolks with the tuna mixture, mayonnaise, and parsley. Season with salt and pepper.

3. Fill each white with a heaping spoonful of the tuna filling. Top with an olive and a sprinkling of tomato and serve with a drizzle of extra-virgin olive oil.

Makes 16

gourmet a go-go's betcha by golly wow eggs

Woo-hoo—this is one wild egg from executive chef Todd Erickson of Gourmet a go-go in Dallas, Texas. One of the most popular catering offerings at Gourmet a go-go is a deviled egg bar, where guests can select their favorite toppings from a spread that includes such things as capers, caviar, prosciutto, and asparagus. The deviled egg is here to stay!

12 hard-cooked eggs, peeled, cut in half, and yolks removed
4 ounces (half an 8-ounce package) cream cheese, softened
2 teaspoons curry powder
2 teaspoons ground ginger
1 1/4 cups unsweetened shredded coconut, toasted
    on a baking sheet in a 350°F oven until light brown
3 tablespoons mayonnaise
1/4 cup minced green onions
Major Grey's or your favorite chutney
1/2 cup fresh cilantro leaves, cut into thin strips

1. In food processor, combine the yolks with the cream cheese, curry powder, ginger, coconut, and mayonnaise and pulse until very smooth. Transfer the mixture to a bowl and fold in the green onions.

2. Fill the whites evenly with the mixture and garnish each egg half with a small spoonful of chutney and a sprinkling of cilantro.

MAKES 24

pesty devils

Prepared pesto is as easy to find as peanut butter in grocery stores these days, and it's good on almost as many things.

1 tablespoon plus 1 teaspoon drained and chopped
  oil-packed sun-dried tomatoes
6 hard-cooked eggs, peeled, cut in half, and yolks
  mashed in a bowl
1/4 cup sour cream
2 tablespoons prepared pesto, plus more for garnish
1/4 teaspoon garlic powder
Salt and black pepper to taste

1. Gently press the sun-dried tomatoes between several layers of paper towel to remove excess oil.

2. Combine the thoroughly mashed yolks with the sour cream and pesto. Stir in the sun-dried tomatoes and garlic powder. Taste, then season with salt and pepper.

3. Fill the whites evenly with the mixture and garnish each egg half with a little dab of pesto.

Makes 12

greek eggs

This recipe from the American Egg Board is based on the classic Greek flavors of feta and olives. Herb-marinated olives would add an interesting twist.

6 hard-cooked eggs, peeled, cut in half, and yolks
  mashed in a bowl
1/4 cup crumbled feta cheese
6 large Kalamata or ripe olives, pitted and chopped
  (about 1/4 cup)

¹/₄ cup mayonnaise

Salt and black pepper to taste

Lemon slivers, olive slices, or fresh oregano sprigs for garnish

1. Combine the thoroughly mashed yolks with the feta, olives and mayonnaise. Taste, then season with salt and pepper.

2. Fill the whites evenly with the mixture and garnish each egg half with a lemon sliver, olive slice, or sprig of oregano.

Makes 12

maharajahs

C hutney is a great seasoning for just about anything (try tossing some in chicken salad sometime). And you can use hot mango chutney instead of Major Grey's for a kick. Fat-free, reduced-fat, or regular plain yogurt all work in this recipe.

6 hard-cooked eggs, peeled, cut in half, and yolks
    mashed in a bowl

2 tablespoons plus 2 teaspoons plain yogurt

1¹/₂ teaspoons curry powder

¹/₂ teaspoon dry mustard

1 tablespoon plus ¹/₂ teaspoon Major Grey's chutney,
    large pieces chopped up

¹/₄ cup chopped cooked chicken

Salt and black pepper to taste

Major Grey's chutney for garnish

1. Combine the thoroughly mashed yolks with the yogurt. Stir in the curry powder, mustard, and chutney, then the chicken. Taste, then season with salt and pepper.

2. Fill the whites evenly with the mixture and garnish each egg half with a dab of chutney.

Makes 12

bella tuscany

I love sun-dried tomatoes packed in olive oil — I eat them right out of the jar. Combine them with rosemary and capers, and you'll want to hop on the next plane to Florence. My intrepid tasters at Elan, where Anthony keeps me as blond as I wanna be, squealed over these eggs, and not much hair got coiffed that day.

1 tablespoon plus 1 teaspoon drained and chopped
    oil-packed sun-dried tomatoes
6 hard-cooked eggs, peeled, cut in half, and yolks
    mashed in a bowl
6 tablespoons sour cream
1 teaspoon fresh lemon juice
1 teaspoon finely chopped fresh rosemary leaves
2 ¹/₂ teaspoons drained and finely chopped capers
¹/₈ teaspoon garlic powder
Salt and black pepper to taste
Slivers of sun-dried tomatoes for garnish

1. Gently press the sun-dried tomatoes between several layers of paper towel to remove excess oil.

2. Combine the thoroughly mashed yolks with the sour cream and lemon juice. Blend in the sun-dried tomatoes, rosemary, capers, and garlic powder. Taste, then season with salt and pepper.

3. Fill the whites evenly with the mixture and garnish each egg half with slivers of sun-dried tomato.

Makes 12

eggstraordinary!

Want to improve your memory? Two eggs provide 100 percent of the daily requirement of choline, which is important for brain development and memory.

dirty martinis

Shake, don't stir, up your cocktail party with these snacks inspired by the trendy drink. Add chopped green olives to the mix if you really like 'em down and dirty. All deviled eggs taste better after they've sat a while in the fridge, but it's really important to let these chill at least 3 or 4 hours, so that the texture firms up.

6 hard-cooked eggs, peeled, cut in half, and yolks
  mashed in a bowl
5 tablespoons mayonnaise
1 1/2 teaspoons vodka
1 tablespoon plus 1 1/2 teaspoons juice from a jar
  of green olives
1/4 teaspoon cayenne pepper
1 1/2 teaspoons finely chopped fresh Italian parsley
Salt and black pepper to taste (lots of pepper is good)
Slices of green olive for garnish

1. Combine the thoroughly mashed yolks with the mayonnaise, vodka, olive juice, cayenne, and parsley. Taste, then season with salt and pepper.

2. Fill the whites evenly with the mixture and garnish each egg half with an olive slice.

Makes 12

eggstraordinary!

Eggs contain all nine essential amino acids.

beelzebub's bloody marys

I t's a drink, it's a snack, it's a great deviled egg. The vodka is optional, and add as much Tabasco as you can stand. The sun-dried tomatoes stand in for tomato juice and provide the best texture if you chop them in the food processor. One of my fearless tasters called these "the naughtiest deviled eggs ever."

6 hard-cooked eggs, peeled, cut in half, and yolks
    mashed in a bowl
1/4 cup mayonnaise
1 tablespoon plus 1/2 teaspoon pureed oil-packed
    sun-dried tomatoes
1 tablespoon prepared horseradish
1 teaspoon Worcestershire sauce
1 tablespoon chopped celery, including leaves
1/2 teaspoon Dijon mustard
1/2 teaspoon celery seeds
1/2 teaspoon Tabasco sauce, or more to taste
1/2 teaspoon vodka (optional)
Salt and black pepper to taste
Chopped celery for garnish

1. Combine the thoroughly mashed yolks with the mayonnaise. Stir in the sun-dried tomatoes, horseradish, Worcestershire, celery, mustard, celery seeds, Tabasco, and vodka, if using. Taste, then season with salt and pepper.

2. Fill the whites evenly with the mixture and garnish each egg half with chopped celery.

Makes 12

magnolia grill's deviled eggs with caviar

B en Barker and his wife, Karen, own Magnolia Grill in Durham, North Carolina. They have perfected the art of lifting Southern favorites to new heights, besides being two of the nicest people on the planet. Ben was voted Best Chef in the Southeast by the James Beard Foundation in 2000, and Karen won *Bon Appétit*'s American Food and Entertaining Award for Best Pastry Chef in 1999, in addition to being nominated for a Beard award several times. They prepared these devils for a James Beard House dinner in New York. The recipe comes from their cookbook, *Not Afraid of Flavor: Recipes from Magnolia Grill*, published in 2000 by the University of North Carolina Press.

12 hard-cooked eggs, peeled, cut in half, and yolks mashed in a bowl

1/2 cup mayonnaise

2 teaspoons Dijon mustard

1/2 teaspoon Worcestershire sauce

1/2 teaspoon Tabasco sauce

2 tablespoons minced fresh chives, plus more for garnish

Salt and black pepper to taste

1 ounce sturgeon caviar (best-quality American or imported)

1. Combine the thoroughly mashed yolks with the mayonnaise until fairly smooth. Add the mustard, Worcestershire, Tabasco, and chives and mix until combined. Season with salt and pepper.

2. Fill the whites evenly with the mixture. The eggs can be made several hours ahead up to this point. Cover tightly with plastic wrap and refrigerate until ready to serve.

3. Right before serving, top each deviled egg with a generous spoonful of caviar and garnish with minced chives.

Makes 24

sharon's hot deviled eggs

My e-mail friend Sharon Christian Aderman in Topeka, Kansas, sent this recipe from her files. Sharon says that she lives in a deviled egg neighborhood: "Every time there is a special occasion or a gathering of neighbors, deviled eggs appear on a plate. When a new baby is born, deviled eggs come to the back door. When a grandparent comes home from the hospital, deviled eggs wait on the kitchen counter. Backyard barbecues, caroling parties, new neighbors—deviled eggs make an appearance."

12 deviled egg halves (use your favorite recipe or try a mild or spicy flavor from this book)
¼ cup (½ stick) butter or margarine
¼ cup all-purpose flour
½ teaspoon salt
¼ teaspoon black pepper
2 cups milk
½ cup dry bread crumbs
½ cup finely shredded sharp cheddar cheese

1. Preheat the oven to 350°F. Arrange the deviled egg halves in a greased 8-inch square baking pan, stuffed sides facing up.

2. In a medium-size heavy saucepan over low heat, melt the butter, then blend in the flour, salt, and pepper. Add the milk and cook, stirring constantly, until thick and smooth. Pour the sauce over the eggs, top evenly with the bread crumbs, then sprinkle on the cheddar. Bake just until the cheese melts. Serve hot.

Makes 6 servings

deviled eggs benedict with sheri's 1-2-3 hollandaise

Hollandaise sauce seems scary to make, but with my friend Sheri's easy technique, it's so simple you'll be spreading it on everything. She says the secret is very cold butter and constant stirring. Also, this sauce is tart, because that's how Sheri likes it. If you're not as fond of lip-puckering flavors, reduce the lemon juice to two tablespoons. The eggs and the sauce can be made up to a day ahead, which makes putting on an elegant brunch easy.

Two 10-ounce packages frozen chopped spinach
Sheri's 1-2-3 Hollandaise (page 75)
12 deviled egg halves (try Ma-Ma's Deviled Eggs,
   Cousin Judy's Deviled Eggs, Springtime Herb Delights,
   or your favorite mildly flavored recipe)
¹/₄ pound thinly sliced prosciutto, coarsely chopped
Paprika for garnish

1. Thaw the spinach in the microwave, then remove as much water as possible by pressing it through a sieve and mashing between paper towels; set aside.

2. Prepare the hollandaise; set aside or refrigerate.

3. When ready to serve, bring the eggs and sauce to room temperature, if they were refrigerated. Spread the thawed dry spinach on a serving platter. Place the deviled eggs on top of the spinach. Sprinkle the chopped prosciutto on top of the eggs. Pour the sauce over them and garnish with a light sprinkling of paprika. Serve immediately.

Makes 6 brunch servings

sheri's 1-2-3 hollandaise

½ cup (1 stick) cold salted butter
2 egg yolks
3 tablespoons fresh lemon juice

1. Cut ¼ cup (½ stick) of the butter into cubes and place in a small heavy saucepan. Place the remaining butter in the freezer. Add the egg yolks and lemon juice to the saucepan. Over very low heat, stir the mixture constantly with a wooden spoon until the butter is melted, 10 to 12 minutes.

2. Remove the butter from the freezer, cut into cubes, and add to the saucepan. Stir constantly until the butter melts and the mixture begins to thicken and turn a rich yellow color, 10 to 15 minutes. (Watch carefully the last few minutes—you'll think it's never going to happen, but it will, all at once.) Hollandaise can be refrigerated, but don't reheat it; let it warm to room temperature and stir to recombine.

Makes about 1 cup

eggstraordinary!

During the time of the czars, Russians celebrated Easter more elaborately than Christmas, giving large amounts of decorated eggs as gifts. Carl Fabergé created the famous jeweled eggs for the royal family from the 1880s through 1917.

hell breaks loose

Welcome to the fires of perdition, where we put the devil back in deviled eggs. Curries from India, jerk flavors from the Caribbean, wasabi of Japan, and Thai chili pastes strike a match in these recipes. Fasten your seat belts.

Zydeco Ya-Yas

The Devil Made Me Do It

Satan's Smokin' Oranges

Horse of a Different Color

Tex-Mex Diablos

Sassy Salsa Swingers

Wasabi-Tuna Eggs

Jammin' Jerk Devils

Buffalo Horns

The Devil Went Down to Georgia

Thai Jungle Princess Eggs

Satan's Sultans

zydeco ya-yas

You can buy Cajun seasoning in the store to make these eggs, but look at the label—many are primarily salt. If you make your own blend, you can really add some flavor—and save up your salt quota for something important, like movie popcorn.

6 hard-cooked eggs, peeled, cut in half, and yolks
  mashed in a bowl
1/4 cup mayonnaise
1 tablespoon plus 2 teaspoons Dijon mustard
1 1/2 teaspoons Salt-Free Cajun Seasoning (recipe follows)
1/4 teaspoon Tabasco sauce, or more to taste
Salt and black pepper to taste
Minced fresh Italian parsley or chives for garnish

1. Combine the thoroughly mashed yolks with the mayonnaise, then stir in the mustard. Stir in the Cajun seasoning and Tabasco. Taste, then season with salt and pepper.

2. Fill the whites evenly with the mixture and garnish each egg half with minced parsley.

Makes 12

salt-free cajun seasoning

Use the freshest dried herbs you can find, and make sure you grab garlic and onion powder, not salt. Feel free to add more cayenne if you like it real hot. You can also rub this seasoning on grilled chicken or fish, or use it to spice up fried chicken or French fries.

1 tablespoon plus 1 1/2 teaspoons paprika
1 heaping tablespoon garlic powder
1 1/2 teaspoons onion powder
1 1/2 teaspoons cayenne pepper

1 1/2 teaspoons dried marjoram
1 1/2 teaspoons dried thyme
1/2 teaspoon hot chili powder

Combine the ingredients. Store in an airtight jar or in the freezer. Because there's no salt in this blend, it may clump, but simply shake to loosen it up before using.

Makes about 1/3 cup

the devil made me do it

This is what I call a deviled egg! When I show up with a plateful, everyone knows they're going to be hot. Be sure to get a fruity, Caribbean-style habanero hot sauce, such as Inner Beauty or, my favorite, a local sauce called Flying Burrito Flounder Juice. A vinegar-based hot sauce like Tabasco will not work at all.

6 hard-cooked eggs, peeled, cut in half, and yolks
  mashed in a bowl
1/4 cup mayonnaise
1 tablespoon Dijon mustard
1 1/4 teaspoons Caribbean-style habanero hot sauce,
  plus more for garnish, if desired
1 teaspoon curry powder
1/4 teaspoon garlic powder
Salt and black pepper to taste

1. Combine the thoroughly mashed yolks with the mayonnaise and mustard. Stir in the hot sauce, curry powder, and garlic powder. Taste, then season with salt and pepper (you may not need any).

2. Fill the whites evenly with the mixture. If you really like it hot, garnish each egg half with a dab more hot sauce.

Makes 12

satan's smokin' oranges

A little sweet and a little hot—okay, a lot hot. Chipotles are smoked jalapeño peppers and they are fiery buggers but in a deep, complex sort of way. Use the canned ones, which come in a flavorful adobo sauce that you can spread liberally on other things. The leftover chipotles keep in the fridge in a plastic bag for several weeks. The hint of sweetness in the salad dressing helps bring out the orange flavor.

6 hard-cooked eggs, peeled, cut in half, and yolks
    mashed in a bowl
2 tablespoons plus 2 teaspoons mayonnaise
2 teaspoons salad dressing, such as Miracle Whip
$^{1}/_{2}$ teaspoon white wine vinegar
$^{1}/_{2}$ teaspoon prepared yellow mustard
1 teaspoon chopped canned chipotles
$^{1}/_{2}$ teaspoon finely grated orange zest, plus more
    for garnish
Salt and black pepper to taste

1. Combine the thoroughly mashed yolks with the mayonnaise, salad dressing, vinegar, and mustard. Blend in the chipotles and orange zest. Taste, then season with salt and pepper.

2. Fill the whites evenly with the mixture and garnish each egg half with a little orange zest.

Makes 12

eggstraordinary!

The practice of dyeing and exchanging eggs predates Christian times as part of the rites of spring.

horse of a different color

A horse is a horse, of course. Unless it's a deviled egg with a lot of wasabi—the fiery Japanese horseradish famous from sushi bars—and conventional horseradish in it. Read the label on the wasabi powder to be sure you get pure Japanese horseradish, with no mustard or other ingredients.

2 teaspoons wasabi powder
6 hard-cooked eggs, peeled, cut in half, and yolks
    mashed in a bowl
2 tablespoons sour cream
2 tablespoons plus 2 teaspoons prepared horseradish
1 teaspoon Dijon mustard
$^1/_2$ teaspoon dry mustard
Salt and black pepper to taste
Fresh Italian parsley leaves for garnish

1. Mix the wasabi powder with just enough water to make a paste and let sit it 15 minutes before using.

2. Combine the thoroughly mashed yolks with the sour cream. Stir in the wasabi paste, horseradish, and both mustards. Taste, then season with salt and pepper.

3. Fill the whites evenly with the mixture and garnish each egg half with a parsley leaf.

Makes 12

eggstraordinary!

To ensure a large family, it was customary for a bride in France to break an egg on the doorstep of her new home.

tex-mex diablos

Fans of smooth fillings, keep turning the pages because this egg is full of lumpy, bumpy good things and plenty of spice. I bet throwing in a few cooked black beans would be tasty, too. *Ay caramba!*

6 hard-cooked eggs, peeled, cut in half, and yolks
   mashed in a bowl

$^1/_4$ cup sour cream

2 tablespoons cooked corn kernels (fresh, canned, or frozen),
   drained well

2 teaspoons hot chili powder

$^1/_2$ teaspoon ground cumin

$^1/_2$ teaspoon garlic powder

$^1/_2$ teaspoon cayenne pepper

2 tablespoons canned chopped green chiles, drained well

2 teaspoons shredded Monterey Jack cheese, plus more
   for garnish

Salt and black pepper to taste

1. Combine the thoroughly mashed yolks with the sour cream. Stir in the corn, chili powder, cumin, garlic powder, cayenne, chiles, and Monterey Jack. Taste, then season with salt and pepper.

2. Fill the whites evenly with the mixture and garnish each egg half with shredded cheese.

Makes 12

sassy salsa swingers

I f you're a wimp, use a mild salsa in this recipe. I went bold and grabbed the hot stuff, of course. Tabasco Chipotle Pepper Sauce is a new variation on the Tabasco theme that adds the rich flavor of smoked jalapeños to the classic heat. If you can't find it, regular Tabasco will work but will lack the interesting twist. Wait until you're ready to serve the eggs before topping with the chips, so they stay crispy.

6 hard-cooked eggs, peeled, cut in half, and yolks
   mashed in a bowl
$1/3$ cup chunky hot salsa, drained
2 teaspoons Tabasco chipotle sauce
1 tablespoon plus 1 teaspoon chopped onion
$1/2$ teaspoon garlic powder
2 teaspoons sour cream
2 teaspoons chopped pickled jalapeños, drained
Salt and black pepper to taste
Coarsely crushed tortilla chips for garnish

1. Combine the thoroughly mashed yolks with the salsa, Tabasco, onion, garlic powder, sour cream, and jalapeños. Taste, then season with salt and pepper.

2. Fill the whites evenly with the mixture, then refrigerate, covered tightly with plastic wrap, until ready to serve.

3. Just before serving, garnish each egg half with crushed tortilla chips.

M A K E S   1 2

eggstraordinary!

There are about 235 million laying hens in the United States, and each hen produces 250 to 300 eggs a year.

wasabi-tuna eggs

Searing green mountain
　　You fire up my deviled eggs.
　　　　Ah, life is tasty.

6 hard-cooked eggs, peeled, cut in half, and yolks
　　mashed in a bowl
1 tablespoon mayonnaise
1/4 cup plus 2 teaspoons drained canned tuna or
　　chopped cooked fresh tuna
1 tablespoon plus 2 teaspoons wasabi powder
1 tablespoon plus 1/2 teaspoon soy sauce
2 teaspoons Dijon mustard
A few drops of toasted sesame oil
1/2 teaspoon cayenne pepper
1 teaspoon peeled and minced fresh ginger
1/2 teaspoon garlic powder
1 teaspoon fresh lemon juice
Salt and black pepper to taste
Pickled ginger slices for garnish

1. Combine the thoroughly mashed yolks and mayonnaise. Stir in the tuna, wasabi powder, soy sauce, mustard, sesame oil, cayenne, fresh ginger, garlic powder, and lemon juice. Taste, then season with salt and pepper. (You may not need much salt because of the soy sauce.)

2. Fill the whites evenly with the mixture and garnish each egg half with a slice of pickled ginger.

Makes 12

jammin' jerk devils

A Red Stripe, a Bob Marley CD, and these tropical devils . . . bliss! You can find Pickapeppa, which is slightly hot but deeply fruity and spicy, in most grocery stores. Be sure to use fresh lime juice from an actual lime, not that stuff in a green plastic fruit-shaped thing.

$^1/_2$ cup chopped cooked chicken

Pickapeppa sauce as needed

6 hard-cooked eggs, peeled, cut in half, and yolks
   mashed in a bowl

2 tablespoons plain yogurt

1 tablespoon fresh lime juice

$^1/_2$ teaspoon ground cinnamon

$^1/_2$ teaspoon ground nutmeg

$^1/_4$ teaspoon ground allspice

2 tablespoons chopped fresh chives

2 $^1/_2$ teaspoons Tabasco sauce

$^1/_2$ teaspoon garlic powder

$^1/_2$ teaspoon dry mustard

Salt and black pepper to taste

1. Place the chicken in a small bowl or on a plate and toss with just enough Pickapeppa sauce to cover. Let sit about 10 minutes, or while you assemble the rest of your ingredients.

2. Combine the thoroughly mashed yolks and yogurt. Stir in the lime juice, cinnamon, nutmeg, allspice, chives, Tabasco, garlic powder, and mustard. Lift the chicken from the Pickapeppa sauce and drain slightly, then add to the mixture. Taste, then season with salt and pepper.

3. Fill the whites evenly with the mixture and garnish each egg half with a dab of Pickapeppa sauce.

Makes 12

buffalo horns

My friend Bridgette once said that she couldn't possibly eat deviled eggs without Buffalo wings on the side. Well, now they're both in one food. Being a North Carolina girl, I used a local Buffalo wing sauce, Texas Pete, but just grab your own favorite. I'm picturing these next to a plate of fried chicken.

1/4 cup chopped cooked chicken
Buffalo wing sauce to cover chicken, plus 5 teaspoons
6 hard-cooked eggs, peeled, cut in half, and yolks mashed in a bowl
1/4 cup (1/2 stick) butter, softened
1/2 teaspoon Tabasco sauce
1 teaspoon chopped celery, plus more for garnish
Salt and black pepper to taste

1. Place the chicken in small bowl and pour in enough Buffalo wing sauce to cover; let sit for at least 5 minutes.

2. Combine the thoroughly mashed yolks with the butter. Stir in the Tabasco and celery. Lift the chicken from the wing sauce and drain slightly, then add to the yolk mixture, along with the remaining 5 teaspoons Buffalo wing sauce. Taste, then season with salt and lots of pepper.

3. Fill the whites evenly with the mixture, garnish each egg half with some chopped celery, and allow to sit at room temperature 15 to 20 minutes before serving to let the flavors develop.

Makes 12

eggstraordinary!

Protein-rich eggs used to be included in shampoos and facial products.

the devil went down to georgia

The sweetest fruit and the hottest pepper . . . peaches and habaneros were just made for each other. Habanero powder is nuclear strength, made from the fieriest peppers known to chileheads like myself—find it at larger supermarkets. I used Sarchi's Peachy Zinger salsa, but there are other peach-flavored salsas you can use. I added my own homemade peach jam—I encourage you to try making jam sometime because it's amazing how much it impresses people besides tasting good—but store bought is fine.

3 tablespoons peach salsa
6 hard-cooked eggs, peeled, cut in half, and yolks
   mashed in a bowl
1/4 cup mayonnaise
1 teaspoon Dijon mustard
1 teaspoon peach jam
1/4 teaspoon habanero powder
Salt and black pepper to taste

1. Place the salsa in a fine-mesh strainer over a bowl to drain well, pressing gently with the back of a spoon to remove excess liquid.
2. Combine the thoroughly mashed yolks with the mayonnaise and mustard. Stir in the drained salsa, jam, and habanero powder. Taste, then season with salt and pepper.
3. Fill the whites evenly with the mixture.

Makes 12

thai jungle princess eggs

I once heard of a whompin' hot Thai dish called Evil Jungle Princess. I can't remember what was in it (the bad-memory curse of middle age), but the name stuck with me, and it's the inspiration for these Asian hotties. You can find fish sauce and chili paste in Asian markets or larger supermarkets. Oh, and what I said about the lime juice before applies here too—people, squeeze it yourself.

12 medium-size shrimp, cooked in boiling water just
    until pink, drained, and peeled

6 hard-cooked eggs, peeled, cut in half,
    and yolks mashed in a bowl

2 tablespoons sour cream

2 teaspoons peeled and minced
    fresh ginger

1 tablespoon plus 1 teaspoon
    Asian chili paste

1 1/2 teaspoons fish sauce

1 tablespoon fresh lime juice

1/2 teaspoon garlic powder

1 tablespoon chopped
    fresh cilantro

Pinch of sugar

Salt and black pepper to taste

Chopped unsalted dry-roasted
    peanuts for garnish

1. Coarsely chop the shrimp; set aside.

2. Combine the thoroughly mashed yolks and sour cream. Stir in the ginger, chili paste, fish sauce, lime juice, garlic powder, cilantro, sugar, and shrimp. Taste, then season with salt and pepper. (You may not need much salt because the fish sauce is salty.)

3. Fill the whites evenly with the mixture and garnish each egg half with chopped peanuts.

Makes 12

satan's sultans

I t's so much fun to browse in ethnic markets, because you discover brand-new flavors for your old favorite dishes. On a trip to a Middle Eastern grocery, I found a jar of this great spread called *ajvar*, which is a mixture of roasted red bell peppers, eggplant, and spices. I used a hot-pepper version in these eggs. Garam masala is a blend of Indian spices and is available in most large supermarkets now — or use your need for it as an excuse to go exploring.

6 hard-cooked eggs, peeled, cut in half, and yolks
    mashed in a bowl
1 tablespoon plus 1 teaspoon sour cream
1 teaspoon Dijon mustard
2 tablespoons hot ajvar spread
1 1/2 teaspoons garam masala
2 1/2 teaspoons Tabasco sauce
1/2 teaspoon red pepper flakes
Salt and black pepper to taste

1. Combine the thoroughly mashed yolks with the sour cream and mustard. Stir in the *ajvar*, garam masala, Tabasco, and red pepper flakes. Taste, then season with salt and black pepper.
2. Fill the whites evenly with the mixture.

Makes 12

eggstraordinary!

Eggshells are great sources of calcium, so toss them on the compost heap instead of in the trash can.

index

Photo by Gene Furr

Debbie Moose is an award-winning freelance writer. She was the food editor and a reporter at the Raleigh *News & Observer* for many years, and she has contributed to several books and magazines. She lives in Raleigh, North Carolina.